# The Rough Places Made Smooth

By

## Margaret S. Russell

Nancy Farr
Baptist Home

Cover photo by Paul Gilmore Photographer.
Cover design by Peg Harvard Graphics.

Printed in the United States of America

**Light For Living PUBLICATIONS**
**PO Box 210**
**Madison, GA 30650**
**Fax 706 342-3380**


**ISBN 0-9627630-6-3**

Life can go on when you realize the rough places can be made smooth, and that "the battle is not yours, but God's," when you can claim this promise: "I will instruct you and teach you."

(Isaiah 45:2; II Chronicles 20:15b; Psalm 32:8a)

# CONTENTS

| | Page |
|---|---|
| Disaster Strikes | 11 |
| Learning To Trust God | 12 |
| God Makes No Mistakes | 14 |
| Spiritual Battles | 15 |
| Satan Tries To Discourage Us | 16 |
| Explaining Death To A Child | 18 |
| Burdens Lifted | 20 |
| God Still Works Miracles | 22 |
| God's Word Never Returns To Him Void | 23 |
| Learning To Walk By Faith | 26 |
| What A Miracle | 27 |
| God Calls Another Loved One | 29 |
| The God Of All Comfort | 31 |
| Children Learn To Pray | 32 |
| Precious Memories | 36 |
| God Wants Full Surrender | 38 |
| Encouraging Others | 40 |
| Never Underestimate The Lord | 42 |
| Children's Friends Always Welcome | 44 |
| Life's Battles Continue, But God Is Greater | 45 |
| Sharing God's Word | 47 |
| God Has All The answers | 48 |
| God's Promised Guidance On Schedule | 49 |

# CONTENTS CONTINUED ——————

| | Page |
|---|---|
| God's Miracles Continue | 52 |
| My Father Is In Charge | 58 |
| Another Opportunity To Share God's Word | 62 |
| More Battles Encountered | 65 |
| Hold Treasures With A Loose Grip | 67 |
| My Testimony | 69 |

# Acknowledgement

Appreciation and thanks are due the following who had a vital part in the production of this book: Bette Gilmore, Elizabeth Maben, Dell Thompson and Margaret Carmichael proofed and evaluated the manuscript at various stages of editing. Paul Gilmore took the picture used in the cover design. Peg Harvard was responsible for making Paul's picture into an attractive cover. Charles Gilmore was responsible for editing and typography.

Light For Living PUBLICATIONS

# FOREWORD

This is a record of God's faithfulness and, appropriately, the testimony of a trusting child—one who found adequate precedent in the Bible.

In a long line of successors the psalmist wrote, "I will remember the works of the Lord" (Psalm 77:11 KJV). The Apostle Paul testified: " Having, therefore, obtained help of God, I continue unto this day, witnessing. . . ." (Acts 26:22 KJV).

Here is an account of a Christian lady, suddenly widowed and left with four children, who obtained help from God; and these pages are her witness.

This chronicle of the loving mercy and unfailing care of a sovereign God brings glory to His Son, Jesus Christ. Your heart will praise Him as you read this true story; and you, also, will be encouraged to trust the faithful God.

I commend these pages to you. They breathe the fragrance of His love and the strength of His sure Word.

Paul R. Van Gorder
Teacher Emeritus
Radio Bible Class

# INTRODUCTION

These pages contain a timely message, especially pertinent to widows, single mothers or anyone in need of encouragement in time of difficulty.

This story of my lifelong friend, Margaret Russell, builds on the Word of God and applies it to personal needs and challenges. There is always the need for testimonies that tie us to the Word of God and encourage us to see Christ and trust Him more in our everyday circumstances. This is that kind of story. It encourages and inspires practical faith—faith to believe that God will provide all of our needs according to His mighty promises.

I have been greatly inspired by the simplicity of Margaret's faith and her complete reliance on the inspiration and authority of the Word of God.

Dell Thompson
Pan American Testament League

**God is faithful,
He will not let you be
tested beyond what
you can bear. . .**

Paraphrase of 1 Corinthians 10:13

# DISASTER STRIKES

It was a cold December morning just before Christmas. Excitement filled the air. This was to be the best Christmas ever—and right after Christmas, we would move into our newly purchased dream home. The phone rang; it was for my husband. A light sleeper, he usually answered the phone on the first ring. Why did he not answer. . . ?

Fear gripped my heart. I stood by the bed for a second, trying to see if he were breathing evenly. Then, I reached down. . . and touched my husband. He wasn't breathing at all! He had gone to sleep and had been ushered into the presence of the Lord as the result of coronary thrombosis. He was only 42 years of age, and I was 34.

I was devastated, knowing that he was beyond any medical attention—any human help whatever! Yet, I was so thankful that he knew Jesus as his Lord and Saviour! Dropping to my knees by our bed, I cried, "Oh my Father, I know You love us. . .what do I do now? Please show me!"

My knowledge of the Lord was quite limited at this point, since I had been a Christian for only a short time. There really wasn't anyone in my life who could sit down and share with me on a one-to-one basis. The years that I faced without my husband drove me to learn at the feet of my Heavenly Father.

# LEARNING TO TRUST GOD

God speaks to us through His written Word. Immediately He brought Psalm 32:8 to my mind: "I will instruct thee and teach thee in the way which thou shalt go: I will guide thee with mine eye" (KJV). This verse became mine; I claimed it for my very own, along with Isaiah 45:2: "I will go before you and make the rough places smooth." Another verse God used to encourage me was II Chronicles 20:15b: "Thus saith the LORD unto you, Be not afraid nor dismayed by reason of this great multitude; for the battle is not yours, but God's" (KJV). I had the joy of constantly claiming these promises, along with many others. As a young widow rearing

**God Protects Widows and Orphans.** four children, our Heavenly Father wanted me to realize that He was not only our Lord and Saviour, but also Husband and Father! "Thy Maker is thine husband; the LORD of hosts is his name. . . ." (Isaiah 54:5 KJV). From Psalm 68:5 in the Amplified Old Testament, I learned that He is "a father of the fatherless, and a judge and protector of the widows. . . ." My Heavenly Father reminded me of these promises when I needed them most.

Although I had been a good church member for twenty years, I had known Jesus Christ as my Lord and Saviour for only two. As I was growing up, however, I read the Bible faithfully and memorized Scripture. Now I was finally allowing my Heavenly Father to use His Word for my good and for His glory! "The Lord is not slow about His promise, as some count slowness, but is patient toward you, not wishing for any to perish but for all to come to repentance" (II Peter 3:9).

**Not all church members really know Jesus Christ as their Saviour and Lord.**

# GOD MAKES NO MISTAKES

In my heart, I knew my Heavenly Father never made mistakes. Nevertheless, I could not help wondering why He took my husband. He was a healthy, robust man who had never really been sick in our thirteen and one-half years of marriage. He was a man who really loved his family. He often told us how much he loved us and showed it in many ways. He made time for play with the children and complimented me on every meal I prepared. He sent long-stemmed red roses to me for every occasion, never forgetting a birthday, anniversary or holiday. Now, the head of our little family was gone. We loved him so much and so desperately needed him! How could we possibly go on without him?

Never again would I hear, "Honey, I love you. . . I appreciate you."

I learned that although we have precious memories, we cannot live in the past, but must live for the present and future. I knew my priority was to train my children in the nurture and admonition of the Lord (Ephesians 6:4 KJV).

My husband had taken care of all the business needs and I took care of the household. However, if any appliance in the house broke down, he had it repaired or replaced within twenty-four hours. Now, the full responsibility was mine. **I soon learned that trust, obedience and patience were included in the valuable training my Heavenly Father had in store for me.**

# SPIRITUAL BATTLES

God called me to rear these children for His glory. The thought of such a tremendous responsibility caused me to tremble. I wanted them taught well at home, in school and in Sunday school and church. Since I was still a new Christian, I did not know how to search the Scriptures properly. The Lord led me to join a Bible-teaching church across town where Dr. Paul R. Van Gorder was pastor.

Many times I would talk to no one but my Heavenly Father about the trials I was facing. He would answer my many questions through my new pastor from the pulpit or through my Sunday school teacher. At that time they knew me only by name. It was at this church that I began learning discernment. I received a good Bible foundation and soon learned how to find the answers for myself. What a delight to study the Scriptures and allow the Holy Spirit to teach me! The children loved the services and we knew we were where the Lord wanted us.

# SATAN TRIES TO DISCOURAGE US

At times the road ahead seemed so difficult. Satan would try to make me think the way was impossible and that I might as well give up. I was very apprehensive of rearing these children alone as a single parent. God knew I could not rear them without Him: "Not that we are adequate in ourselves to consider anything as coming from ourselves, but our adequacy is from God" (II Corinthians 3:5). But God also knew what He could do through me, if I would only permit Him to have His way in my life.

Daily, God reminded me that He was going before me smoothing the rough places, and that the battle was not mine, but HIS! I had to learn to trust Him fully and live one day at a time—actually, one moment at a time. I had to learn to keep my eyes ever on Jesus, constantly claiming His promises. I took as mine Isaiah 54:13: "All thy children shall be taught of the LORD; and great shall be the peace of thy children" (KJV) and Philippians 4:13: "I can do all things through Him who strengthens me."

"Lord Jesus," I prayed, "above everything, I want my children to know YOU as their Lord and Saviour and live in the power of Your Resurrection."

---

**ALL THY CHILDREN SHALL BE TAUGHT OF THE LORD.**
(Isaiah 54:13 KJV)

# EXPLAINING DEATH TO A CHILD

## How do you explain death to a little child?

At the funeral home, the two little ones begged me to wake up Daddy. Even later, when we took fresh flowers to the grave, It was difficult for them to understand why they couldn't see Daddy.

"Lord," I prayed, "how do I tell my little ones their Daddy won't be coming back. It is so hard, Father, when I am hurting beyond words to try to tell them about death."

They hugged me as if they would never let go, while tears streamed down their faces, and they asked: "Why doesn't Daddy come home? We love him and we know he loves us. Why did Jesus take him? We need Daddy!"

"Lord," I prayed, "this is the hardest question I will ever have to answer for them. It is hard for me to understand. Speak through me to them."

Psalm 23:4 came to my mind: "Even though I walk through the valley of the shadow of death, I fear no evil; for Thou art with me. . . ."

While driving down the street one sunny day, we noticed a large van approaching us. I called attention to this as I pulled over and told the children to watch the shadow the van would cast on us as it passed by. Then the Lord allowed me to explain that when Jesus is our Lord and Saviour, He is like that shadow. The van did not hit us; only the shadow, and it did not hurt at all!

As a family, we enjoyed fishing and the Lord allowed me to use this to teach the children. We were fishing along the shoreline of the lake in the shade of some beautiful trees. Here we could enjoy the trees and flowers and the cool waters on a scorching summer day, without fear of being sun-burned. I explained, "We only passed through the shadows. Jesus is that Shadow of death, that prevents any harm coming to us when He takes us Home to Himself. Daddy had gone to sleep and when he woke up, he was on the most beautiful shore, called Heaven. Although we will be separated for a while, Jesus has provided the WAY for us to be together again with him one day."

# BURDENS LIFTED

When my husband died, the children were 11, 8, 5, and 3. As I looked at my circumstances, the days ahead seemed long, dark and so hard to bear. Trials occurred continuously. At times, they were so great and so frequent, I felt like a drowning person. Every time I came up for air, I went under again. It was a tremendous spiritual battle.

The Lord brought Luke 22:31, 32 to my mind, where He said to Peter: "Simon, Simon, behold, Satan has demanded permission to sift you like wheat; but I have prayed for you, that your faith may not fail; and you, when once you have turned again, strengthen your brothers."

By substituting my name for Simon Peter's, these verses became mine. Just think, Jesus prayed for me . . . my faith could not fail! "He is able to save forever those who draw near to God through Him, since He always lives to make intercession for them. . . . Christ did not enter a holy place made with hands, a mere copy of the true one, but into heaven itself, now to appear in the presence of God for us" (Hebrews 7:25; 9:24). How encouraging! Here was hope and comfort!

I learned that when the way gets too rough, our Lord carries us in His arms: "Like a shepherd He will tend His flock. In His arm He will gather the lambs, and carry them in His bosom" (Isaiah 40:11).

I quickly found that some people consider widows easy prey in financial matters. Some wanted to charge exorbitant legal fees for handling estate business. Others tried to overcharge for repair jobs. But the Lord's provision for us was always sufficient and often more. I learned that our trials, burdens and disappointments are God's opportunities for great blessing. I had to learn to trust and be obedient in all areas of life—every minute of the day. These lessons were hard for me to learn, but God was patient and faithful.

# GOD STILL WORKS MIRACLES!

On the morning my husband passed away, he had an appointment to sign the mortgage insurance papers for our newly purchased home. Since this appointment was never filled, this huge debt now became my responsibility. He had life insurance, but there were the children to rear and educate. I certainly did not want to go to work, as the children definitely needed me more than we needed the extra money—or a larger house.

"Help, Lord," I cried "Debt frightens me—show me what to do."

He reminded me of Hebrews 13:5-6: "Let your character be free from the love of money, being content with what you have, for He Himself has said, **'I WILL NEVER DESERT YOU, NOR WILL I EVER FORSAKE YOU,'** so that we confidently say, **'THE LORD IS MY HELPER, I WILL NOT BE AFRAID. WHAT SHALL MAN DO TO ME? '"**

God also spoke to me about my fear of debt through Psalm 72:12: "He will deliver the needy when he cries for help, the afflicted also, and him who has no helper"; through Isaiah 8:13: "It is the

LORD of hosts whom you should regard as holy. And He shall be your fear, and He shall be your dread"; and through Jeremiah 33:3: "Call to Me, and I will answer you, and I will tell you great and mighty things, which you do not know." How reassuring were all these promises!

# GOD'S WORD NEVER RETURNS TO HIM VOID

As the result of my memorizing so many Scripture verses when I was growing up, God brought these verses to my mind when I needed them. This was His way of speaking to me personally. He often reminded me of Isaiah 55:11: "So shall My Word be that goeth forth out of My mouth: it shall not return unto Me void, but it shall accomplish that which I please, and it shall prosper in the thing whereto I sent it" (KJV).

If I were not sure how the verse was worded, I learned to use a good concordance. God had given me a great hunger and thirst for His Word, and I did not want to miss anything my Lord was saying to me. I knew He had brought me to this place to teach me something special and I did not want any of these valuable lessons to escape me.

The children and I, along with my mother, who lived with us, moved into our new home. We continued to pray about the mortgage payments. We claimed these promises from II Chronicles 20: "O our God, wilt Thou not judge them? For we are powerless before this great multitude who are coming against us; nor do we know what to do, but our eyes are on Thee" (v. 12). "Thus says the LORD to you, 'Do not fear or be dismayed because of this great multitude, for the battle is not yours but God's'" (v. 15b). "You need not fight in this battle; station yourselves, stand and see the salvation of the LORD on your behalf" (v. 17). We learned that God delights in taking care of the little things, as well as the overwhelming things—not only the difficulties, but also the impossibilities! "Behold, I am the LORD, the God of all flesh; is anything too difficult for Me?" (Jeremiah 32:27).

> **Nothing is ever too difficult for the Lord.**

My husband, a dental surgeon, was a tender-hearted man. He allowed people to pay their bills as they were able and consequently had more money in accounts receivable than in the bank. The majority of his patients paid their bills on time. A large number of the other patients paid their bills soon after his death. As the result, the mortgage was completely paid off within six months! God gets all the glory!

I could have responded in an entirely different way to the Lord's timing. Satan would have wanted me to argue with the Lord that if my husband had been allowed to live just one more day, then all of the stress over the mortgage payments would have been eliminated. God reminded me that the battle was not mine, but His—that He would go before me and make the rough places smooth. These circumstances increased my confidence in God. I was learning to trust Him regardless of how bleak or difficult the situation. I learned that God delights in performing miracles.

**God delights in performing miracles for YOU.**

# LEARNING TO WALK
# BY FAITH

Many times the way was not opened until the very last moment when the need became urgent. I could relate to Peter when he was released from prison in Acts 12:7-10. The iron gate at the prison opened only when Peter walked up to it on his way to freedom—his only way of escape.

Also, in Joshua 3, when the Children of Israel were crossing the Jordan River, God did not roll back the swollen waters until the priests who were carrying the Ark of the Lord first put their feet in the water. They had to have faith to do this. And this was what my Heavenly Father wanted to teach me. I had to learn to walk by faith; to take God at His Word—which is to read His Word, believe IT and act on IT! "My God shall supply all your need according to His riches in glory by Christ Jesus" (Philippians 4:19 KJV).

> **To walk by faith, you must take God at His Word, then step into the water expecting Him to open up a way for you to get through.**

# WHAT A MIRACLE!

One particular time, my clothes dryer broke down. If my husband had been living, the dryer would have been repaired or replaced by the following day! You see, I had been taken care of very well by my husband.

Now I had to learn to let God take care of my family and me. The Lord was teaching us to wait for His timing.

I called a service repairman to check the dryer. He said it needed a new motor which would have to be ordered. It would be about three weeks before he could have it working again. This happened during the winter months when it was too cold and wet to dry clothes outside. Then one of the children developed a virus which made him nauseated and much too weak for me to leave him to go to a laundromat.

By this time, we were very low on fresh sheets and towels. I claimed God's promises: "Is anything too hard for the LORD?" (Genesis 18:14 KJV); and "If you ask Me anything in My name, I will do it" (John 14:14). I prayed that God's Name would be glorified while I washed a load of sheets and put them in the dryer, turned it on—AND IT WORKED! God honored His Word! To God be the Glory! He is still in the miracle-performing business. He is interested in everything we do!

I caught up on the laundry, but not before the service repairman came with the new motor. Hearing the dryer running, he said, "You've had someone else to repair it!"

"Yes", I answered, "**the Lord repaired it!**"

"For he will deliver the needy when he cries for help, the afflicted also, and him who has no helper" (Psalm 72:12). That clothes dryer gave me many years of good service before any part of it had to be replaced! I learned and taught my children that God is interested in everything that comes into our lives. Sometimes He allows situations where we have to look up to HIM—and HIM alone. We can no longer depend on anyone or anything else.

Oh, the valuable lessons God was teaching us! I learned when the trials were the greatest, Jesus was the closest to us. No trial or hardship is allowed to come to one of His children without first touching Him.

# GOD CALLS ANOTHER LOVED ONE

My mother and I had always been very close. She was so much help, and we loved her dearly. We shared God's Word and prayed together. It was always a pleasure and blessing to be with her. Then, on Mother's Day, only three and one-half years after my husband's death, God called her home. It seemed that the Lord was removing all my earthly props, so I would have to put all my trust in Him.

"What do you want me to learn from this sorrow, Father? " I prayed. He led me to Isaiah 51:2: "I called him alone, and blessed him, and increased him" (KJV). I learned this was the place where God wanted me, and I knew I had much to learn in this area.

Jesus, Himself, set an example of being alone with God when He commanded: "When you pray, go into your inner room, and when you have shut your door, pray to your Father who is in secret, and your Father who sees in secret will repay you" (Matthew 6:6). I learned that one of the things which is pleasing to the Heavenly Father is spending time alone with Him. I read and studied about

Moses, Joshua, Jacob, Elijah, Elisha, Daniel, David, and Paul.

I saw how God enabled them to carry out their God-assigned tasks. He would do the same for me! The same POWER God used in and through these men is STILL AVAILABLE. "I pray that the eyes of your heart may be enlightened, so that you may know what is the hope of His calling, what are the riches of the glory of His inheritance in the saints, and what is the surpassing greatness of His power toward us who believe. These are in accordance with the working of the strength of His might which He brought about in Christ, when He raised Him from the dead, and seated Him at His right hand in the heavenly places" (Ephesians 1:18-20).

GOD'S POWER IS AVAILABLE FOR YOU.

# THE GOD OF ALL COMFORT

When I was sad and needed comfort, my Lord comforted me from His Word: "Comfort, O Comfort My people" (Isaiah 40:1) "Blessed be the God and Father of our Lord Jesus Christ, the Father of mercies and God of all comfort; who comforts us in all our affliction so that we may be able to comfort those who are in any affliction with the comfort with which we ourselves are comforted by God" (II Corinthains 1:3-4). I said, "Lord, You will have to enable me for this as I need comforting."

Then, I learned that God allows sorrows, trials, testings, temptations, heartaches and difficulties in our lives for a purpose: They help us to become more intimately acquainted with Jesus, experience the power of His resurrection and accept Him as our Comforter. Then we can identify with others in order to comfort them. God was building my character, allowing my faith to grow, and making me a more mature Christian.

# CHILDREN LEARN TO PRAY

The early morning hours (from 5:00 to 6:00) were the best times for my personal devotions. There were several reasons for this early encounter. One was, I wanted to begin each day with Jesus while my mind was fresh. Another reason, there were no interruptions while the children were still asleep and a very important reason was, I was up when the children began their day. This meant so much to them.

Shortly after the death of my husband, I overslept one morning. Since the children were accustomed to my being up early, they walked into my bedroom holding hands. They thought they would find me dead. When I saw the fear on their faces and remembered the helpless feeling of finding a loved one dead, I tried to prevent that from happening again.

At times during my devotions, I would read entire chapters. Sometimes, I would read only one or two verses. Regardless of how much or how little I read, I would allow the Holy Spirit to speak to me and explain God's Word. These times were precious and priceless as I sat at my Lord's feet and learned of Him. I learned to lean on Him and to trust Him fully. Our family devotions were held at night. It was heartwarming to see the children taking God at His Word, learning to pray, and looking to Him for guidance in their lives. Jesus was in our midst! "For where two or three have gathered together in MY NAME [emphasis added], there I am in their midst" (Matthew 18:20).

Knowing there was absolutely nothing too hard for the Lord, the children and I often claimed Jeremiah 32:27: "Behold, I am the LORD, the God of all flesh; is anything too difficult for Me?" We learned to pray about everything—even, seemingly, the most minute. Shopping, good parking places when we went anywhere, protection while driving, school grades and sewing. Every purchase which was made, and every bill which we received were always on our prayer list. We learned that God was more interested in all our needs than we were!

Every month, I made a list of the money that was needed for all the bills and everyday living. The children and I would pray in detail over each need, claiming the Lord's promises as our Provider. He never failed once! We knew God wanted us to spend His money wisely. His part came first, and we lived on what was left. God supplied all our needs! "But my God shall supply all your need according to his riches in glory by Christ Jesus" (Philippians 4:19 KJV).

Although I was somewhat apprehensive about renting, I decided to keep the house where we had lived for ten years for rental property. Almost immediately after we moved, a young Christian couple called about renting; and I couldn't have asked for more perfect tenants. If there were any needed repairs, the man did them, then told me what he had done, and many times refused reimbursement! Other attempts to provide income were not so successful, however.

Because professional men were not required to pay Social Security for themselves until almost a year after my husband's death, Social Security income was virtually eliminated for us—only the years when my husband was in military service as an officer during World War II counted.

Then when I was told that a dental practice could not, at that time, be sold after the death of the doctor, back to my knees I went: "Lord give me wisdom in handling this. Show me a dedicated Christian business man with whom I can talk about these problems—someone who can advise me on what to do."

"That particular morning, at 5:00 A. M. during my devotions, I was reading Psalm 118 and pouring out my heart to the Lord. Just when I needed the answer, there it was in verse 8! "It is better to trust in the Lord than to put confidence in man" (KJV). What clearer direction could I need than that?

The Lord led me to sell the equipment in my husband's office and keep the building to rent. That rental income, along with rent from the rental house, enabled us to live without using the majority of the insurance money.

> **It is better to trust in the Lord than to put confidence in man.**
> **Psalm 118:8**

# PRECIOUS MEMORIES

For many years my Lord gave me the privilege of staying home with my children. I had the joy of being there when they needed me and when I needed them. Many times when we were in the car together as a family, one would begin singing and all joined in, some in harmony. These were delightful times. When we finished one song, someone would start another. As the result, we learned many hymns and three of the four children eventually became soloists. We also played many games on long trips. One of the most memorable was, "Who am I?"—describing Bible characters. On this one, I really had to do some research, between trips, to keep up with my children. This was an education in itself!

God led me to enroll the children in private Christian schools. This was another difficult lesson to learn. The oldest would be in a boarding high school 250 miles from home, located just west of Asheville, NC. Bible conferences were held there during the summer months.

We, as a family, were attending a conference there one summer. Just before one of the services began, my oldest daughter came to me and said, "Mother, there is one opening in the school and a long waiting list. I've been praying to come to school here."

Believe me, this struck me like a dagger in my heart! Was God calling me to give up my children also? Was our little family to be split up again? A few years earlier, this same daughter had told me she felt the Lord's calling to prepare for the mission field. I was pleased, but that was a long time out in the future. I did not want her to leave home yet, not right now! "Please Lord, I want my children to have a good education, but do they have to leave home at such an early age? "

As my child looked at me for an affirmative answer, the Lord gave me the grace to say, "Let's pray about it!" And pray I did! After pouring out my heart to the Lord, I said, "Lord, it just isn't fair!"

We went on to the service, but I don't remember who the speaker was; and at that particular time, I couldn't have cared less. I sat there in the meeting hall thinking about "poor ole me" in my party of pity-parties. It was sad going to the conference that year without my mother, who had gone to be with the Lord only three months before. This was such a short time after my husband's death. Did the Lord want me to send my child to a boarding school in another city so soon? "Why me, Lord? Please have mercy! I can't take anymore!"

# GOD WANTS FULL SURRENDER

The Lord patiently waited for me to calm down. Finally, as the service was closing, He reminded me of John 13:7: "What I do you do not realize now, but you shall understand hereafter."

Then I remembered Proverbs 3:5-6: "Trust in the LORD with all thine heart; and lean not unto thine own understanding. In all thy ways acknowledge him, and he shall direct thy paths" (KJV). God allowed me to see that He could take much better care of my children **in His will**, than I could **out of His will.**

**Learning To Commit Our Wills and Our Ways To The Lord**

I said, "Not my will, Lord, but Yours." My Father was teaching me that I had to surrender ALL my possessions to Him. This meant my will and my most precious possession—my children! I learned to let go of everything my God had entrusted to me.

My daughter and I filled out the application forms for her enrollment and left the results to the Lord—knowing whichever way He led would be the right direction. We claimed Psalm 32:8: "I will instruct thee and teach thee in the way which thou shalt go; I will guide thee with mine eye" (KJV).

A verse which really hit home was Philippians 2:14: "Do all things without murmurings and disputings. . ." (KJV). Then I was convicted by I Timothy 5:8: "If anyone does not provide for his own, and especially for those of his own household, he has denied the faith, and is worse than an unbeliever." I said, "Lord, I don't know anyone who does not provide food, clothing and shelter for their family."

He showed me that although that is important, few people were providing spiritual training. This is much more important than any other provision because this involves ETERNITY! My Father wanted me to train my children so they would be able to teach others, also: "You therefore, my son, be strong in the grace that is in Christ Jesus. And the things which you have heard from me in the presence of many witnesses, these entrust to faithful men, who will be able to teach others also" (II Timothy 2:1-2).

My daughter got that one opening at the boarding school and the other children followed later. "Thank you, Father, for your guidance and your patience with me." Jeremiah 33:3 is true: "Call to Me, and I will answer you, and I will tell you great and mighty things, which you do not know."

# ENCOURAGING OTHERS

The Lord provided for all four children to attend Christian schools. Two were now in boarding high school and the other two in Christian day school. During this time, a lady mentioned that she and her husband were praying for enough money to send their one child to the Christian day school. She was told that I had all of mine in Christian schools. The lady asked me what kind of work my husband was in, that we could afford to have all of our children in private schools.

> You Can Trust God To Supply Your Need.

"I'm a widow," I answered, and her eyes seemed to pop out of her head.

Breathlessly, she exclaimed, "You're a widow and have four children in private schools! Where do you work?"

I calmly replied, "I don't work outside the home."

I shared with her what God was doing in our lives and told her we were learning to trust Him for everything worth having. I also told how we were learning to commit our wills and our ways to Him. I explained that our Lord wants us to live by faith, so we must be willing to allow God to work in and through us.

The next time I saw that lady, she told me her child was attending the Christian school. "Is anything too hard for the LORD?" (Genesis 18:14 KJV.)

# NEVER UNDERESTIMATE THE LORD

At the beginning of one school year, we were much in prayer for enough money to pay tuition for all four. The oldest was in college. Two were in Christian high school in North Carolina. My son was still in Christian day school. We did not want to use the insurance money, which was reserved for college. And, we definitely did not want to go ahead of the Lord's leading. If the money were not supplied, we would take it as from the Lord that it was His will for the three younger children to attend public schools.

Although many people still owed on dental bills, we did not pressure them. We knew they would pay as they were able. While waiting for God's guidance, we continued with the packing for boarding school. We were $600.00 short of the total amount of tuition.

The day arrived for the girls to leave and everything was ready except the money. God reminded me that the battle was not mine, but His. We knew the Lord would provide our every need, so we continued in prayer.

The Lord led us back to II Chronicles 20, reading and claiming again verses 15 and 17: "Ye shall not need to fight in this battle: set yourselves, stand ye still, and see the salvation of the LORD. . . : fear not, nor be dismayed; tomorrow go out against them: for the LORD will be with you" (KJV). Then we knew it was definitely God's will for the girls to go to the Christian high school.

**God Wanted To Increase Our Faith**

As they left, I told them the money would be there in time for registration. Our Lord had not failed us yet! He had promised He would supply all our need—not all our wants, but all our need (Philippians 4:19).

The very next day, someone who owed us money called and wanted to pay $600.00 toward the amount they owed. My children and I had talked to no one about this need except the Lord! The money arrived at the school in time for registration! God gets all the glory!

On two different occasions after that, when we wanted to be sure of the Lord's will, we prayed about specific amounts of money needed. We wanted ONLY God's will. God answered by sending TEN TIMES the amount needed! One was from overpayment on taxes. The other was the sale of some real estate! God gets all the praise!

# CHILDREN'S FRIENDS ALWAYS WELCOME

For the next fifteen years, on weekends, Christmas holidays, and sometimes entire summers, we had missionary children and other students from the schools in our home. At times, I never knew how many people would be there for a meal until it was time to prepare it. We loved it! Many of the parents dropped by when they were home from the mission field. All were welcomed and we enjoyed every one of them, remembering Hebrews 13:2: "Be not forgetful to entertain strangers: for thereby some have entertained angels unawares" (KJV).

It was interesting and exciting to hear what God was doing for and through these people as they told of their experiences on the various mission fields. Little did I dream at that time of ever visiting some of these places as the mother of a missionary.

# LIFE'S BATTLES CONTINUE—
# BUT GOD IS GREATER!

Later, when I had one daughter in college and the financial needs were pressing, the Lord led me to go to work. I worked for eighteen years before taking early retirement.

While there, the trials continued. Again I claimed Luke 22:31-32. Satan did not want to give up, but knowing Jesus had prayed for me and the Holy Spirit was making intercession for me, how could I fail?

I was further encouraged by Romans 8:26-28: "The Spirit also helps our weakness; for we do not know how to pray as we should, but the Spirit Himself intercedes for us with groanings too deep for words; and He who searches the hearts knows what the mind of the Spirit is, because He intercedes for the saints according to the will of God. And we know that God causes ALL [emphasis added] things to work together for good to those who love God, to those who are called according to His purpose."

Paul declared; "I am crucified with Christ: nevertheless I live; yet not I, but Christ liveth in me: and the life which I now live in the flesh I live **BY THE FAITH OF THE SON OF GOD** [emphasis added], Who loved me, and gave Himself for me" (Galatians 2:20 KJV). Think of that! I am living—not by my faith—but—BY THE **FAITH OF JESUS!** He knows what He can do through me.

My Lord wanted me to learn how to trust Him even more. He wanted to increase my faith, as when he instructed Simon Peter: "Put out into the deep water and let down your nets for a catch" (Luke 5:4).

I also realized that my Lord was calling me to be His witness in my situation: "You are my witnesses,' declares the LORD; —'and my servant whom I have chosen. . .'" (Isaiah 43:10); and again, "You are witnesses. . ." (I Thessalonians 2:10). I often prayed, "Set a guard, O LORD, over my mouth; Keep watch over the door of my lips" (Psalm 141:3), and "Let the words of my mouth, and the meditation of my heart, be acceptable in Thy sight, O LORD, my strength and my redeemer" (Psalm 19:14 KJV).

# SHARING GOD'S WORD

While working, I was asked by many of my co-workers for advice as they shared their problems at lunchtime or when we rode together to work. How good it was to tell them of God's love for them, and I praised the Lord for every opportunity He gave me to witness for Him.

Most of the problems we discussed concerned disagreements between them and their spouse. I shared with each of them a plan my husband and I agreed on early in our marriage. I explained, "No two people can live together without an occasional disagreement. The secret is to keep it between the two of you, while praying and working it out. Don't tell anyone else about it—not even your own parents. In this way, the disagreement is quickly forgotten. If you tell anyone else, it is remembered by both you and the other person. Often a small disagreement is blown out of proportion by others."

> **Don't Allow Disagreements With Your Spouse To Be Blown Out Of Proportion By Complaining To Others.**

# GOD HAS ALL THE ANSWERS

I learned that the Lord wants each of us to study His Word, to "Be diligent to present yourself approved to God as a workman who does not need to be ashamed, handling accurately the word of truth" (II Timothy 2:15).

I have also learned that my Father has the answer for our every problem; you will find the answer in His Book. I am still learning; I have not graduated yet—I won't have that honor until I stand before the Lord! He can use us for His glory as long as we trust and obey. We are never too young or too old to be used by our Lord. I've found age doesn't mean a thing to my Lord. "Let no one look down on your youthfulness, but rather in speech, conduct, love, faith and purity, show yourself an example of those who believe," (1 Timothy 4:12) and, "They will still yield fruit in old age" (Psalm 92:14). I may have retired from my eight-hour-a-day job, but there is no retirement from being a child of God!

**Remember, you are never too young, or too old to be used by the Lord.**

# GOD'S PROMISED GUIDANCE ON SCHEDULE

Shortly after I began working, two of the children and I went to the graduation exercise for my son at the Christian grade school he attended. As we approached the expressway on our return home, someone rammed our car from the back. The impact pushed us out into the traffic, badly damaging our car and injuring us. Two days later we had to be in Asheville, N. C. for the graduation of one of my daughters from the Christian boarding school she was attending.

I faced a dilemma. With the whiplash I had received, how was I going to drive? And what would I drive? I certainly did not want to miss the Baccalaureate service or my daughter's graduation.

Back to my knees I went. "Lord," I prayed, "with my sore, stiff neck, it will be impossible to drive. I don't want to do anything foolish and endanger lives. The girls will be coming home for the summer, from high school and college, with all their luggage. We need a large car. Show me what to do."

Immediately, the Lord reminded me of two verses in Isaiah: "I will go before you and make the rough places smooth. . ." (45:2), and "He gives strength to the weary, and to him who lacks might He increases power. . ." (40:29).

The salesman from the company where I had purchased the car, and where it was being repaired, called and said a demonstrator car was available for me to use. In the meantime, my daughters had prayer meetings going on for me at the college and high school. I drove to Asheville without any problems with my neck! Oh, the power of prayer! What a Saviour!

There were many unusual opportunities for sharing God's Word. One weekend when my son was home from college, we were in a hurry to finish Sunday dinner and get his clothes packed. The telephone rang. When I answered the phone, the caller asked for one of my daughters. It just so happened that the daughter she asked for would not be home until the following weekend.

The girl sounded so disappointed. Normally, I would have asked her to call back later, since our time was running so short; but responding to her disappointment, I asked: "Is there anything I can do for you?

"She answered, "I want to accept Jesus as my Saviour, and my parents won't let me."

What an opportunity! I shared God's Word with her, giving the plan of salvation. The amazing thing was, this girl had dialed the wrong number! She thought she had the residence of someone by the same name as my daughter. What a Saviour! He can even use mistakes for His glory!

After spending so much time with the girl, my son and I still had time to enjoy a leisurely Sunday dinner before he had to return to school.

Another time, I was busy in the kitchen and had just put a banana pudding topped with a lovely meringue in the oven, when I saw someone coming to the door. I thought, "I can't leave that pudding in the oven over five minutes, or it will be ruined- so I just won't answer the door." But the Lord brought to my mind that this was a lost person ringing my doorbell; so I said, "Lord, You take care of that banana pudding, and I will go to the door."

The lady belonged to a cult and I counseled with her for about thirty minutes, showing her God's Word and giving her some gospel tracts.

When she left, I checked on the banana pudding—and it was beautiful! The Lord is interested in every little detail in the lives of His children—even a banana pudding for dessert!

# GOD'S MIRACLES CONTINUE

Several years later, my oldest daughter was serving as a missionary in the Philippines. Of course, I wanted to fly over to see her and her family. By this time my other children were established in their own careers. My son, who was working with an airline in Chicago, called to say he could get a pass for me. How exciting! I had just enough vacation time to go for a busy two-week visit.

The day arrived for me to leave. My bags were packed and I was ecstatic with joy. I was looking forward to seeing my daughter, my son-in-law and my three grandchildren whom I had not seen in a year. Everything was ready to go. My flight was to leave at 5:30 P. M. from Atlanta. My two daughters who lived in Atlanta were leaving their offices early to take me to the airport.

Then, around 8:00 A. M. on the day of the flight, my son called to say the tickets had not yet come through. His supervisor had told him they had been approved; so we could not understand the delay. My son said that he would check on them again, and if they had come through, he would send them by a friend, who was flying into Atlanta in time for me to leave at the appointed time. He told me to go to a certain counter, promising the passes would be there.

"Lord," I prayed, "what a test of patience—but I know nothing is impossible with you."

Sure enough, the passes were where my son said they would be, and I left at the appointed time! "Thank You, Father, for Your many blessings, Your faithfulness, Your provision and Your encouragement."

The Lord allowed me to share His Word with several passengers. I wanted to take advantage of every opportunity.

My flight took me to the International Airport in Manila, 600 miles north of where my daughter lived on Mindanao Island. They had made arrangements for some of their friends to meet my flight in Manila and take me to their local missionary guest house. There I could rest a few hours before my next flight later in the morning.

Unfortunately, when I arrived at midnight, I could not find their friends. Since the airport closed at midnight, there was no choice but to take a taxi to the guest house. I did not know that taking a taxi was not safe for a lady traveling alone, even during the daytime.

Normally a taxi trip from the airport to the guest house took about one hour, but my driver had trouble finding the address of the guest house and stopped many times to ask directions. At every stop I was viewed with great curiosity, especially at that time in the night. Jesus reminded me that He was with me wherever I went.

I arrived safely at the guest house at 3:00 A. M., thankful that I had had plenty of time to witness to the taxi driver. Only an hour and one-half later, I had to leave the guest house to go to the domestic airport to catch the plane to Mindanao Island.

My son-in-law, a pilot, would meet me and fly me to their home in Nasuli in time for breakfast with my family. It was then I learned that many foreign women had been robbed by taxi drivers in Manila. How devastating it would be to lose your passport, airline tickets, money and clothing in a foreign country! My Lord again reminded me that the battle was not mine, but His! All of us—my daughter, son-in-law, three grandchildren and I—thanked the Lord again for His protection and provision.

Shortly after my arrival that morning, my daughter, a nurse, had to fly out to see a patient in a remote village on a mountain. I went along, although I had had very little sleep in the past thirty-six hours. My daughter finished with her patient and we boarded the small aircraft to return home. She cautioned, "Mother, you had better close your eyes when we take off," to which I responded, "why? I like to see where I'm going."

Then I saw why! The runway was extremely short. If we were not airborne by the time we reached the end of the runway, we would drop off the mountain! I learned that God sends superb pilots to the mission field!

Over the next several years, the Lord provided for me to fly to the Philippines to visit my daughter and her family many times. On one return trip home, while checking in at the ticket counter, I was told my name was not on the confirmed list and that I could not get a boarding pass. I assured the ticket agent that the confirmation had been made, as I looked over the counter to see the list for myself. Reading the names upside down, I found mine and pointed it out him. He apologized, but still would not give me a boarding pass.

Silently, I prayed, "Help, Lord, You know what to do."

At that moment another ticket agent, with whom I had shared the Gospel on a previous trip, walked up. We began talking as if we had known each other for years—even asking about each other's family.

All this time, I had not moved from where I was standing and was watching the first ticket agent out of the corner of one eye. He shuffled some papers for a few seconds, then said, "Ma'am, do you want in smoking or non-smoking?"

"Window, non-smoking, please," I replied, and continued talking with the lady. When I received my boarding pass, I thanked the agent, wished him a good day, handed him a Gospel tract and went on my way.

I arrived in the waiting room with only a few minutes to spare before boarding the plane for the long flight across the Pacific. The lady ticket agent ran up to me with a letter to her sister in the States and asked if I would mind mailing it for her. Then she grabbed my boarding pass for the crowded tourist section and said she would be right back.

In the meantime, people were boarding; and I said, "Lord, I'm trusting You."

Within seconds, the ticket agent ran back with a boarding pass for the executive section, saying, "No one will be using these seats."

She knew I would like to stretch out! There were three empty seats together, and I got to use them all for eighteen hours—all the way from Manila to San Francisco! Oh, how our Father loves each one of us! I remembered I Peter 5:7: "Casting all your anxiety upon Him, because He cares for you."

# MY FATHER IS IN CHARGE

On another flight out of Manila, we landed in Guam. After discharging some passengers and refueling, we were on our way again. Just as the pilot picked up speed to take off, he stopped suddenly and announced that we had a flat tire. We were encouraged to remain calm while he taxied back to the airport to replace the tire. Then suddenly, the pilot exclaimed, "Everyone go to the center door and get off this plane immediately—do not stop to get your hand luggage!"

All 250 passengers scrambled for the one door to which the long steps had been rolled for our escape. The ground crew was motioning for everyone to RUSH, RUSH, RUSH! Some people began to panic, pushing and shoving as we descended the steps. I knew my Father was in control. He had promised to be with me wherever I went, and His peace and calmness enabled me to help others: "Peace I leave with you; My Peace I give to you; not as the world gives, do I give to you. Let not your heart be troubled, nor let it be fearful" (John 14:27).

The tires on the plane were on fire, the landing gear had been stripped and the runway torn up! We were told to stay in the tiny airport until another plane from Manila could pick us up. The Lord gave me this opportunity to talk with many people and share His Word. Not one person was injured.

At 3:00 A. M. we were taken by bus to a beautiful Guam hotel for the remainder of the night and for breakfast. My lovely room with a balcony was overlooking the gorgeous Pacific. It was absolutely breath-taking. The only bad thing was, all our luggage was still on the plane. We were wearing all the clothes we had. It was sixteen hours before another plane came to pick us up for the long flight across the Pacific and HOME.

None of my children knew I was on that plane. When they heard about the trouble on the news, they checked with the airline to find out if I was a passenger. My name was not listed, since there had been several mix-ups in getting on the flight in Manila. I remained calm through the entire ordeal, until I arrived in San Francisco and called home. When I heard my daughter's voice, I broke down; and she knew immediately that I had been a passenger on that plane. Again I thanked my Lord for His protection and provision and claimed salvation for every person involved in taking care of the passengers.

On one flight to the Philippines, my luggage did not arrive in Manila when I did at midnight. With my scheduled early morning flight to Mindanao Island, there was no possibility of getting my luggage in time. I trusted the Lord to keep all the luggage and contents safe.

There were Christmas gifts for my daughter, son-in-law and grandchildren—repair parts for their stove and jeep, a new toaster oven, fresh fruit and vegetables unavailable there. There was also a limited amount of clothing, plus one item used by all the missionaries at the center—a Sears catalog. I filled out the necessary papers to recover my luggage and went on my way—600 miles south of Manila. My only change of clothing was in my tote bag.

When I arrived in Nasuli, my daughter and family, along with many missionaries at the center, were at the hangar to meet me, . Stepping off the plane, I held up my handbag and totebag and announced, "This is my luggage."

Everyone knew immediately my luggage had gone astray. My grandchildren responded, "No gifts? " Someone asked if the Sears catalog was in the lost luggage! I had to borrow clothes until mine arrived.

A couple of days later, a missionary had to go to Manila. He agreed to check on my luggage at the airport. It had arrived, but he was told that the baggage could not be released without my passport.

The missionary said, "I don't have Mrs. Russell's passport, but here is mine."

The baggage clerk responded, "That is sufficient."

I got my luggage!

# ANOTHER OPPORTUNITY TO SHARE GOD'S WORD

Upon my return from one trip to the Philippines, my sister-in-law called, inviting me to go to England with her. This was a trip for airline personnel and their families.

I told her that I had been out of the office for four weeks and did not see how I could leave again so soon. Although I had more vacation time available, I did not want to take advantage of my employer. Besides that, the work had just piled in for our department.

However, I decided to brush up on the history of England. The more I thought about a visit there, the more interesting the trip became. So, I made it a matter of prayer!

I asked the Lord that if He could use me to go to England for His Glory on this trip, to open up the way, and if not, to block it. I left the trip in the hands of the Lord and went about tackling the heavy load of work still flooding my office.

Two weeks later, my supervisor wanted me to ask the employees in my department if they would take their vacations at that particular time. All of the information we had received on the computer tapes was incorrect. There would be absolutely nothing for our department to do for two weeks while the corrections were being made! I relayed this information to the employees and asked if they would take early vacations. Their answer was unanimous: "IN APRIL? NOT NOW!"

Going to the my supervisor's office, I told him of their response. Then I talked to him about the trip to England and said, "I need a vacation."

His response was, "Go, and have a good time."

I thanked my Lord, packed my bags, armed myself with Gospel tracts and off to England I went!

On one particular tour in London, our group was in Saint Paul's Cathedral and the guide was explaining some paintings. One was a painting of Jesus knocking at a door covered with vines. The guide said, "This is the way it is with us when Jesus knocks at the door of our hearts. If we don't respond, it won't be long until we will be unable to hear Him."

I was at the back of the group but worked my way up to the guide as we were on our way to another painting. I said, "You sound like a born-again Christian."

He answered, "No, lady, but I wish I were."

Handing him a gospel tract, "God's Plan of Salvation," I replied, "Here is the answer right here," and quoted several Scripture verses to him before we arrived at the next painting. I thanked the Lord for sending me to England. I asked Him to give me more openings to share His Word. Most of all, I wanted Him to get the glory.

It was April—cold and raining the entire time we were there. This didn't bother me; I love the rain. Besides that, I was on a mission for my Lord and I was in England!

Every time I went into a shop, I would greet the shopkeeper with a cheerful "Good Morning," or "Good Afternoon." The response was always the same, "How can you be so cheerful on a day like this?" What an opportunity to witness! Those Gospel tracts were always handy and I had a delightful time passing them out and sharing God's Word.

# MORE BATTLES ENCOUNTERED

After twenty years in our beautiful home, the time came to sell. There were so many wonderful memories wrapped up in this house. The children grew up here. While in high school and college, their choirs came for dinner whenever they were on tour through Atlanta. Weekly Bible classes were held here, as we could easily entertain large groups. But, as we prayed, we became convinced that it was time to move. Five burglaries, resulting in the loss of personal, sentimental items, confirmed my decision. Many beautiful, expensive gifts from my husband and parents could never be replaced.

Another theft which really hurt was at church. Someone picked up the Bible my husband had given me. This was a tear-stained Bible I used in rearing my children. It contained notes I had written during my devotions over the years.

The burglaries brought back an old pain—FEAR. This started with a burglary in an apartment building when my oldest child was a baby. It occurred during World War II, while my husband was overseas.

Although the burglar did not reach our apartment, the intrusion brought fear that remained with me for many years. It was not until I had accepted Jesus as Lord and Saviour that I could release that fear to Him.

Before that time, I was so afraid to be alone at night with a baby that I let my imagination run wild. I thought: "what if that intruder comes back and kidnaps my baby? What if the house burns and we are trapped!"

Now, as His child, my Lord reminded me of II Corinthians 10:5. "Casting down imaginations, and every high thing that exalteth itself against the knowledge of God, and bringing into captivity every thought to the obedience of Christ. . ." (KJV). My Father assured me of His presence, so I never lost any sleep. "In peace I will both lie down and sleep, for Thou alone, O LORD, dost make me to dwell in safety" (Psalm 4:8). I could now pray for the thieves. My Jesus died for them too!

# HOLD TREASURES WITH A LOOSE GRIP

"Lord," I prayed, "what do you want me to learn from these burglaries?"

Immediately, He reminded me of Matthew 6:19-21: "Do not lay up for yourselves treasures upon earth, where moth and rust destroy, and where thieves break in and steal. But lay up for yourselves treasures in heaven, where neither moth nor rust destroys, and where thieves do not break in or steal; for where your treasure is, there will your heart be also."

My Lord was teaching me to hold on to my possessions loosely, regardless of the sentimental value. The last verse hit hard: "For where your treasure is, there will your heart be also," (v. 21); and following it into my mind was Exodus 20:3: "You shall have no other gods before Me." "Lord," I cried, "after all You've done for me, surely I don't have any gods before You!"

He reminded me of a hobby I had for more than twenty years—china painting. I realized that when I finished one piece, I could hardly wait to begin another. Because of the time involved, I was making my hobby a god  and grieving the Holy Spirit. "Do not grieve the Holy Spirit of God, by whom you were sealed for the day of redemption" (Ephesians 4:30). I needed to clarify my priorities!

I saw how easy it is to allow the adversary to creep in unaware. My Lord reminded me of I Peter 5:7-8: "Casting all your anxiety upon Him, because He cares for you. Be of sober spirit, be on the alert.  Your adversary, the devil prowls about like a roaring lion, seeking someone to devour."

I had been spending too much time on this hobby; and confessed the sin of this love to my Lord, as we are told to do in I John 1:9: "If we confess our sins, He is faithful and righteous to forgive us our sins and to cleanse us from all unrighteousness."

I asked the Lord to remove the love I had for my hobby, if it became a hindrance to me, and He did. Later, however, He gave the hobby back to me, along with a beautiful illustration of the Christian life, in a pair of table lamps I had painted.

Much time had been spent on painting and firing them  three different times up to 1500 degrees F. The Lord showed me that He longs to

teach His children great lessons about Himself—
trials that bring us forth as gold which is a glory to
HIM! He gives us a deeper understanding of WHO
HE is as we are willing to walk with Him through the
difficulties of life.

I can now paint china again, without any
feeling of guilt, and enjoy it—when I have the time
to do so!

# MY TESTIMONY

## I was a good church member, but lost.

> "I never knew you, depart from me. . ."
> (Matthew 7:23).
>
> "Whosoever shall call upon the name of the Lord shall be saved."
> (Acts 2:21).

When I ask people if they know Jesus Christ
as their Lord and Saviour, many respond with "Oh,
I'm a charter member of my church" ; or "I keep
the Ten Commandments";or "I've been attending
church all my life"; or "I joined the church at an
early age."

I also joined the church at an early age—twelve years old, in fact. I was searching, but for what, I was not sure. I thought being a member of the church was the thing to do!

Reading the Bible and memorizing Scripture verses became a daily habit. I lived a good life, not wanting to do anything to hurt my parents, whom I loved dearly. I did not want to do anything that would mar our good family name. I attended church regularly and sang in the choir. My sister and I often sang duets in church and at church functions. When I was an older teenager, my pastor asked me to teach a children's Sunday school class.

I heard many sound gospel sermons, but by clinging to my "good life" and "good works," I refused to allow the Holy Spirit an opportunity to speak to me personally. Oh, I knew Jesus died for sinners, but I had never considered myself bad enough for Jesus to have to die for me!

Time went on! I married a wonderful man and we had four lovely children. We attended church regularly and the children loved Sunday school. As a family, we began attending Bible Conferences, west of Asheville, NC. It was there that I allowed the Holy Spirit to search my heart.

Many verses of Scripture stood out in my mind. One was Revelation 2:7: "He who has an ear, let him hear what the Spirit says to the churches." God allowed me to see that I had been closing my ears to the Holy Spirit's teaching for twenty years. I had ignored what He desired for me to know.

Another verse was James 2:10: "Whoever keeps the whole law and yet stumbles in one point, he has become guilty of all." This verse really hit home even with my "good life and all my good works," I knew I had to be guilty in at least one point—but what?

> **God spoke to me through His written Word.**

Pride kept me from talking with anyone about my spiritual condition. After all these years, how could I face anyone if they found out I was not a Christian? What would people think of me? After all, I was a church member and a Sunday School teacher!

At one of the services at the Bible conference, I heard a message on Matthew 25:21: "Well done, thou good and faithful servant" (KJV). I was under such conviction that I went to my room after the service. Falling on my face before the Lord, I said, "Oh God, look at my good life, my wonderful works. I'm a good wife, good mother, a church member. I've been baptized. If I were to die right now, You would say to me, 'Well done, good and faithful servant,' wouldn't You?'"

The Lord immediately brought Matthew 7:23 to my mind: "I never knew you: depart from me, ye that work iniquity." What an awakening! What an eye-opener!

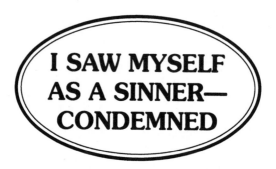

**I SAW MYSELF AS A SINNER— CONDEMNED**

For the first time in my life, I saw myself a sinner—condemned! The Lord allowed me to see myself standing—not at the Judgment Seat of Christ—but at the Great White Throne Judgment along with all those horrible sinners. I, who had lived such a good life was no better than they.

"Lord," I cried, "what must I do to be saved?"

Immediately, Jesus brought Acts 2:21 to my mind: "Whosoever shall call upon the name of the Lord shall be saved" (KJV). The Lord showed me that I was included in that "whosoever," and that He died for me personally. My sin drove the nails in His hands and feet, and His Blood was shed for me! It was not the sin of commission, but the sin of **omission!** It wasn't what I had done, but what I **hadn't done.** I was turning my back on God's plan.

I was refusing Jesus! I was rejecting what God had sent His Only Begotten Son to earth for—to die at Calvary in my place.

In essence, I was telling God, "I have a better plan!"

I wanted to go to Heaven **my way**, on **my terms!** God brought to mind verses of grave meaning: "Verily, verily, I say unto you, he that entereth not by the door into the sheepfold, but climbeth up some other way, the same is a thief and a robber" (John 10:1 KJV); and John 10:7, where Jesus said, "Verily, verily, I say unto you, I AM [emphasis added] the door of the sheep" (KJV); and clearest of all—John 14:6, in which Jesus said, "I AM the WAY, and the TRUTH and the LIFE [emphasis added]; No one comes to the Father, but through Me." If I had died without accepting Jesus, this Gift-of-Gifts, God would have turned His back on me—Jesus was THE ONLY ONE who could pay that penalty for me!

For the first time, I saw that Jesus died for me personally at Calvary. My sins were nailed to the Cross with Him. I accepted God's plan of salvation and He gave me His assurance that I was His child in Romans 8:1: "There is therefore now no condemnation to them which are in Christ Jesus, who walk not after the flesh, but after the Spirit" (KJV).

God let me see that I died **with Him**, was buried **with Him**, and rose again to eternal life **with Him**: "I have been crucified with Christ; and it is no longer I who live, but, Christ lives in me; and the life which I now live in the flesh I live by faith in the Son of God, who loved me, and delivered Himself up for me" (Galatians 2:20). I live not by my faith, but by the faith of the Son of God! He even promised His guidance, His wisdom and His presence. And that He would never, never leave me! (Hebrews 13:5). Praise the Lord—WHAT A SAVIOUR!

**There is therefore now no condemnation for those who are in Christ Jesus. . . The Spirit of life in Christ Jesus has set you free. . .**

Romans 8:1-2

I praise the Lord for His GREAT LOVE for me, HIS FAITHFULNESS to me and HIS PATIENCE with me. I am thankful that He allowed me to memorize scripture at an early age. God has shown me many times that Isaiah 55:11 is true, that His Word never fails: "So shall my word be that goeth forth out of my mouth, it shall not return unto me void, but it shall accomplish that which I please, and it shall prosper in the thing whereto I sent it" (KJV). And I have personally experienced that "the Lord is not slow about His promise, as some count slowness, but is patient toward you, not wishing for any to perish but for all to come to repentance" (II Peter 3:9).

## God's Word accomplishes His purpose

I am amazed and so thankful for my Lord's constant protection, as I look back over the years before I was saved. One Fourth of July, as a young teenager, I was riding with a group of young people in an open truck to a picnic. On a very sharp curve, I lost my balance and would have fallen off but for the protective hand of the Lord. A cousin grabbed me just in time. Twice I almost drowned while swimming. Then our house burned one night while our family was asleep. We escaped only seconds before the house caved in.

One month before my high school graduation, there was a very heavy rain storm. The river between our house and the school overflowed, washing away the bridges. The only way I could get to school was to use our rowboat to cross the swollen river. It was a cold and rainy day. I was dressed for the weather, with a heavy coat, rain cape and boots. I carried an armful of books and booklets to be turned in before I could get credit to graduate. My brother rowed the boat. The swift waters pushed us down stream. My brother told me to catch hold of some overhanging tree branches to steady the boat. I definitely knew better, but I stood up and grabbed the branches—and out I went, books and all! My dad, who was standing on the bank started after me, but I yelled to him that I was all right. I swam with one hand, holding on to my books, and didn't lose anything despite my heavy clothing. I missed school that day, but did graduate with my class.

Years later, after I turned my life over to the Lord and He called me to teach a Sunday school class, I used these experiences from my pre-

Christian years. "If any man's work is burned up," Paul wrote, "he shall suffer loss; but he himself shall be saved, yet so as through fire" (I Corinthians 3:15). For example, I can relate to the crossing of the Jordan River during flood time as recorded in Joshua 3. When God parted the water of the Jordan, the river was swollen and the waters very swift (Joshua 3:15). I can identify with this scene that challenged the faith of the Children of Israel.

I have been purchased with a great price—the precious BLOOD of JESUS—and my body is His temple. He is now living His life through me. "Do you not know," the Apostle Paul teaches in I Corinthians 6:19-20, "that your body

> **I have been purchased with the blood of Jesus.**

is a temple of the Holy Spirit who is in you, whom you have from God, and that you are not your own? For you have been bought with a price: therefore glorify God in your body." What a GREAT PRICE JESUS paid in order for me to live eternally with Him! And He made this GIFT of gifts available to me and everyone else: "For by grace you have been saved through faith; and that not of yourselves, it is the GIFT of GOD; not as a result of works, that no one should boast" (Ephesians 2:8-9). All we have to do is accept it as our very own!

He gave me the privilege of **KNOWING**—not just hoping—that I have eternal life. Actually KNOWING that I have eternal life **NOW**, while still alive! My Heavenly Father tells us in I John 5:13: "These things I have written to you who believe in the name of the Son of God, in order that you may know that you have eternal life." I have been "accepted in the Beloved" (Ephesians 1:6 KJV) and "sealed with that Holy Spirit of Promise" (Ephesians 1:13 KJV). He wants me to spend eternity with Him—He loves me! **WHAT A SAVIOUR!**

I have learned to claim many, many promises for my very own, including these encouraging ones: "Not that we are sufficient of ourselves to think any thing as of ourselves; but our sufficiency is of God" (II Corinthians 3:5 KJV); "I can do all things through Him who strengthens me" (Philippians 4:13)." I knew that my Father keeps ALL of His Promises. I still remember the promises, but have forgotten many of the trials and hardships!

I learned that, when God removes the husband and father, Satan tries to take over that authority and life indeed becomes a daily battle. When I faced trials, God gave direction by bringing me to a place where I had to face the question, "Was I going to try to handle this alone or allow Him to take care of the situation through me?" "For apart from me, you can do nothing" (John 15:5). When I allowed Jesus to handle my trials, He was building my character and I was becoming a more mature Christian. I knew that "No temptation has overtaken you but such as is common to man; and God is faithful, who will not allow you to be tempted beyond what you are able, but with the temptation will provide the WAY [emphasis added] of escape also, that you may be able to endure it" (I Corinthians 10:13). Jesus said, "I AM THE WAY" [emphasis added] (John 14:6). Jesus is always our way of escape when we belong to Him.

It was obvious that the Lord had many special lessons He wanted to teach me through these sorrows and trials. I wanted to learn everything! So, I threw myself on His mercy, desiring that it would return to me in ways best suited to my needs. I prayed for a real hunger for His Word and He honored my request.

The Lord has taught me to count my blessings. He showed me that regardless of how bad our circumstances appear, we can always find some-one much worse off. I had to learn to keep my eyes on Jesus and not on my feelings or my circum-stances. Jesus became my constant companion. He is my Life.

Today, all of my children have known Jesus Christ as their Lord and Saviour for many years. God gets all the praise! One is already with the Lord. The other three are making Him known in their daily walk with Him.

My greatest desire was to rear these children entrusted to me by my Heavenly Father to know Christ and the Power of His Resurrection. I claimed His promise in Isaiah 54:13. "ALL [emphasis added] thy children shall be taught of the LORD, and great shall be the peace of thy children" (KJV). I learned that my Lord never gives us any task without first enabling us, and He is that ENABLER: "Faithful is he that calleth you, who also will do it" (I Thessalonians 5:24 KJV). TO GOD BE THE GLORY!

**Indeed life has been a battle with many rough places, but it belonged to my Heav-enly Father. He has taken full responsi-bility—making the rough places smooth and has led me all the way—as He promised.**

# Christian
# Growth
# Resource
# Material

**LIGHT** for Living Publications
P. O. BOX 210
FAX 706 342-3380  Madison, GA  30650-0210  USA

*Books that light up your life*

English Resource CATALOG

## Books By Charles Gilmore

# The Way To Life & How To Live It ————— $5.95

This book explains how man was created a spiritual being to live in a physical body. It reveals how man was given a human spirit for a dwelling place for God Himself. God was forced to vacate that human spirit when man sinned, so man became alienated from God. Thus, separated from God, man entered into a new realm—spiritual death. This book goes beyond spiritual death to explain how you can enter a whole new realm of life through spiritual birth.

Spiritual birth is just the beginning of the Christian life. To really enjoy that life and fulfill God's purpose, a Christian must mature by growing in grace and knowledge of Jesus Christ. This book tells you how. Every seeker of truth should read this book. Every Christian should have a copy for reference and guidance for living the Christian life.

# Handbook For Living The Christian Life ————— $4.95

In simple easy-to-understand language, it reveals what really happens when a person receives Jesus Christ as personal Savior. It also explains how a new Christian can grow and mature in Christ, learn how to pray, understand the Bible, choose new friends and find the peace and joy Christ promised. A supplement on physical love relationships deals with such subjects as: love, sex, marriage, divorce, remarriage and homosexuality. Answers 40 questions vital to Christian living. Every Christian can benefit from the information found in this handbook.

# Get Dressed For Battle ————— $2.50

When my wife, Bette, and I discovered how occult practices, supernatural abilities, curses, etc. could be passed down from one generation to another, we had a clue that freed some held in bondage for years. Contrary to what we had been taught, we learned that becoming a Christian does not automatically make us immune to demonic attack. In fact, Satan often intensifies his activity when a person trusts Christ. This book is not an exhaustive study on the subject. Rather, it reveals some truth that brought freedom to those in bondage.

Although we are Christians and soldiers in the Lord's Army, we must live in enemy territory. God has provided armor for our protection and equipment for battle, but we must put it on. Without it you are sure to become a casualty, so. . .GET DRESSED FOR BATTLE.

# Books by George B. Eager

George Eager, founder and director of Mailbox Club International, has been writing books and Bible studies for many years. They have been translated into numerous languages, with millions distributed around the world. For 15 years he edited a paper called TEEN TALK, sent to 100,000 young people each quarter. He has spoken to hundreds of thousands of young people in more than 3800 meetings. But his ministry is not limited to young people. His practical Biblical solutions to life's problems have proven effective for both the young and the old of this generation.

We are offering some of George Eager's most popular books because we know that you will benefit from this resource. Please find order form on next page.

## ❋ Winning Children To Christ _____ **$5.95**

For parents, teachers, counselors, pastors, children's workers.

A HOW TO book. Tells you HOW TO: get your message across; give an invitation; counsel effectively; lead a child to Christ; evangelize children through the mail; teach victory to children.
Paperback, 180 pages.

## ❋ Love Dating and Marriage _____ **$5.95**

For teens and single adults.

For teens and singles. Gives Biblical principles on love, dating and marriage in plain understandable language. Loaded with terrific stories that young people can identify with and learn from. 160 pages, paperback.

## ❋ New Life Discipleship Series _____ **$5.95**

For group study. All ages.

This 13-week study course explains simply and clearly why every person needs to be born again. It tells how to experience the new birth. Daily Bible readings and devotional guide help the student obtain a happy, fruitful walk with the Lord.
Ideal for small group study. 160 pages, spiral bound.

This audio Bible study is designed to inform and enlighten, so you can appropriate the victory that has already been provided through the Lord Jesus Christ.

Victory In Demonic Crisis
By Charles F. Gilmore
Light for Living
P.O. BOX 210 - Madison, GA 30650
Do not copy for resale

$ 4⁵⁰
US CURRENCY

Answers many questions, such as:

✸ Can a Christian be demon possessed?

✸ What are the symptons of demonic activity?

✸ Do believers have authority to cast out demons?

✸ How can I be victorious in demonic crisis?

Classic book on prayer by Cam Thompson

Over 400,000 in print.

## Master Secrets of Prayer ———————————— $5.95

This unique book on prayer was born out of twenty years experience in the school of prayer. Each secret principle was tested and proven true during a lifetime of trusting God for every need. The author really lived in the spirit of prayer and his life had an impact on all who knew him. He defined prayer as, "The spreading out of our helplessness and that of others in the name of the Lord Jesus Christ before the loving eyes of a Father who KNOWS, UNDERSTANDS, CARES and ANSWERS." It was Cam's desire that these gleanings of a lifetime be used by God to inspire Christians everywhere to greater adventures in prayer.

Recommended by many Christian leaders such as, Dr.Charles Stanley, In Touch Ministries. Often quoted by prominent authors such as, Ruth Graham, (wife of Billy Graham).

Use mail order form

# MAIL ORDER FORM

It is our desire to provide books, Bible studies and other resource material to help you grow and mature in Christ. If you have other specific needs not offered here, please let us know.

| | how many | price ea. | total |
|---|---|---|---|
| The Way To Life & How To Live It | | $5.95 | |
| Handbook For Living The Christian Life | | $4.95 | |
| Get Dressed For Battle | | $2.50 | |
| Master Secrets Of Prayer | | $5.95 | |
| Victory In Demonic Crisis { audio cassette | | $4.50 | |
| Winning Children To Christ | | $5.95 | |
| Love, Dating and Marriage | | $5.95 | |
| New Life Discipleship | | $5.95 | |
| SUB TOTAL | | | |
| FOR POSTAGE, ADD $1.00 First book, .75 each additional book. | | | |
| Foreign ship/handling | | | |
| GRAND TOTAL | | | |

For foreign shipping / handling, add $3.00 first book, $2.00 each additional book. Pay in US $.

**Make check or money order payable to Light For Living PUBLICATIONS**

MAIL TO

Please print your name and address on mailing label below.

Light For Living Publications
PO Box 210
Madison, GA 30650-0210 USA

**BOOKS**

To

# YOU CAN STUDY A BIBLE COURSE AT HOME AND RECEIVE A CERTIFICATE

Just complete this application and mail to address below.
✓ Check the subject that interests you. Knowledge of your age, interests and Bible background helps us to enroll you in a series that will be of greatest benefit.

## SUBJECTS

- ☐ A simple study on SALVATION
- ☐ Beginners for children
- ☐ Beginners for adults
- ☐ Practical Christian Living
- ☐ The New Life in Christ
- ☐ Doctrinal studies
- ☐ Soul Winning
- ☐ Love, Dating and Marriage
- ☐ other _____

✓ the appropriate box.

| AGE | EDUCATION |
|-----|-----------|
| ☐ Adult | ☐ Hi School Grad. |
| ☐ Teen | ☐ College Grad. |
|  | ☐ Bible Sch. Grad. |

☐ If younger, write your age in this box.

## There is no time limit. Study at your own pace.

The cost of providing the Bible studies comes from contributions. You may contribute as you are able.

Tax exempt receipts are issued for all amounts above the cost of material you receive.

✓ LANGUAGE ?

☐ English ☐ Spanish ☐ Portuguese ☐ Korean ☐ Russian

**FAX SERVICE**  You may enroll by fax. Fill out this enrollment and fax it to 706 342-3380.

These Bible studies could greatly enrich your life. To receive your first booklet, print your name and address on label below. The next booklet will be mailed upon receipt of your answer sheet.

MAIL TO

Print your name and address

LIGHT For LIVING BIBLE STUDIES
P. O. BOX 210
Madison, GA 30650 USA

To _____

clip here and mail

## The Rough Places Made Smooth

## Order this book for a friend

If this book has been a blessing to you, perhaps you would like to send one to a friend.

We will include this gift certificate and mail the book direct to your friend. Just sign below and put your friend's name and address on mailing label on other side.

Gift

*Given by*

_____

Certificate

## MAIL ORDER

**$4.95** each book
**$1.00** postage

**$5.95** Postpaid USA

FAX 706 342-3380

Payable to

Mail to

Light For Living PUBLICATIONS
P O Box 210
Madison, GA 30650-0210 USA

## The Rough Places Made Smooth

Outside USA, add $2.00 each. ☐ Pay in USA currency.
Write or fax for quantity prices.

|  | How many | Price ea. | Total |
|---|---|---|---|
| Books |  | **$5.95** |  |
| Foreign shipment |  | **$2.00** |  |
| Total |  |  |  |
| GA residents add 6% sales tax. |  |  |  |
| Grand total US $ enclosed |  |  |  |

Print or type name and address on mailing label below.

**BOOK**

_____
Name

_____
Address

_____